Get Cooking in the Classroom

Recipes to Promote Healthy Cooking and Nutrition in Primary Schools

Sally Brown

and

Kate Morris

Brilliant
PUBLICATIONS

Contents

Recipes

How to Use this Book

This book has been designed to help you meet the new criteria. It provides:

❖ A step-by-step approach specifically following the National Curriculum targets for cooking
❖ Development of skills in food handling
❖ Understanding of the part food plays in the world around us
❖ A range of cross-curricular links.

All the recipes have been created to enable children to develop food preparation skills as they progress through the school, whether you cook every week and use these as a foundation to get you started or whether you cook once a term. The recipes are easily adapted and amended to introduce a wider range of ingredients. They can be redesigned to incorporate different nutritional requirements. This means you will be able to respond to requests from the catering team to introduce an unfamiliar food, or include ingredients familiar to your children.

We have based the development of skills for each Key Stage (as listed below) on a combination of the progression framework published by The D&T Association and the recently updated UK Core Food Competences (see www.nutrition.org.uk).

Key Stage 1 (5–7 years)

Skills you can look to develop include: pull, juice, peel, spread, shape, rolling pin, mix and stir, whisk, rub-in, spoon, measure with spoons, use simple fractions, cut-out (with cutter or knife), grate soft foods, snip, thread, cutting low resistance foods with table knife, follow simple recipes.

| Dips (3 different ones to make) | Wrap Sandwich (Design Your Own) | Tomato and Cheese Scones | Highland Pudding (Cranachan) | Ginger and Pineapple Cheesecake |

Lower Key Stage 2 (7–9 years)

Reinforce skills from Key Stage 1 and look to develop the following: using a garlic press, swivel peeler, shaping and moulding, mixing with hand mixer, two spoon method, measuring jug, digital scales, using cutters, grating foods, snipping, threading, cutting medium resistance foods, claw grip (ie cutting tomatoes/cooked potatoes), blender, toaster and hob.

| Potato Omelette (Frittata) | Savoury Bread and Butter Pudding | Saucy Fish Pie | Fruit Crumble (Design Your Own) | Peach and Cherry Upside-down Cake |

How to Use this Book (cont)

Step-by-step photographs show how little the children need to have in front of them for each of the stages. This reduces the risk of over zealous or premature additions of ingredients and optimises the chances of great results! Have everything set out ready on a separate table close to hand so you can add and remove ingredients and equipment as they are needed. And we always recommend you have spare equipment and ingredients, where possible, of everything for that 'just in case' moment. There's even a photograph of the finished dish so you can see what you are aiming for.

For each recipe we have identified an additional D&T task along with ideas for linking it to two additional curriculum areas, to bring the cooking activity into more of the children's learning. We are sure you will have a huge range of ideas too.

Introducing new ingredients
The children you are teaching may never have seen some of the ingredients you introduce them to, or have no idea of what goes into the food they eat. This is an opportunity to amaze them with the magic of cooking.

You can use their individual work mat as a tasting plate, placing small samples of the ingredients for them to handle and taste as they add them to the recipe.

Lead by example
As teachers, why do we suggest making your own mixture with the children?
1. You should lead by example
2. Some children learn better by following/copying rather than by instruction
3. If a child drops their mixture you can offer to replace it with yours
4. You will have a version to taste together and discuss.

You could also make one before the lesson (store appropriately) to show what it should look like. Or you can show the photograph of the finished dish provided at the bottom of each recipe sheet.

Nutrition and Health (cont)

You may like to use the Eatwell Plate to help you.

This is a visual representation of the proportions of the five food groups that we should be aiming for in a balanced diet. We like to think that the purple section should be put to one side and considered as only an occasional part of a balanced diet.

Knowledge and understanding of healthy nutrition should be built up cumulatively over the year groups. Start with simple messages like five a day and help children identify foods that would meet that target. Then move on to introducing the food groups. Then move on to more sophisticated concepts such as Protein, Carbohydrates, Vitamins and Minerals, their roles in our healthy diets and the needs of different groups of people, eg children, adults and vegetarians.

The key messages are:

❖ Eating well means you should eat foods from the four main food groups.

❖ Eat foods in starchy foods group (yellow on the Eatwell Plate). Eat at least five portions of fruit and vegetables (green) every day – mostly vegetables.

❖ Eat moderate amounts of foods in the meat (pink) and dairy (blue) groups every day.

❖ Eat only occasionally foods in the high fat and high sugar group (purple).

Activity idea

Give out large paper plates and pictures of foods and drinks cut from magazines advertising/ printed off illustration web sites. Get the children to put the pictures into the four healthy food groups and remove the foods that appear in the high fat/high sugar group. Then they can stick the healthy foods and drinks they like onto the plates.

Getting Started: what you need to know

School policy

Is there already a school food policy document and does this cover practical food work in the classroom? Does someone in the school have any experience or expertise to tap into? The recipes include some specific food and equipment handling skills, for example, and there may be safety procedures already in writing covering this. Is there a food champion with interest or expertise in the school, or perhaps a parent who can help you set up and get started? Check whether there is a risk assessment for cooking in school. Your local education authority may have produced one to help you.

Discuss the policy of the helping of children to handle food and equipment. For example, guiding a child's hand when using a grater or shadowing a child as they use a sharp knife. It is not dissimilar to helping a child get the correct grip on a tennis racquet. Raise these issues before you start with the SLT and other staff or volunteers who will be cooking.

Be mindful of over enthusiastic parent/adult helpers who 'do' rather than 'show', otherwise it becomes the adult's achievement and not the child's.

If you have a school kitchen, discuss your plans with the Head Chef or food provider. There may be opportunities to use some of the expertise from the kitchen, consolidate orders with suppliers to save time and money, and perhaps have access to the oven or refrigeration. Policies will vary for different schools and regions.

Providing ingredients

The provision of the ingredients for your practical food work needs careful consideration. Can you supply all the ingredients at school? Can you ask for a contribution from the parents to help cover some or all of the cost? By supplying all the ingredients you ensure the quality, hygiene and availability for the session so no child has to miss out. If children are providing their own ingredients then you don't know where it was bought or when, or how it has been stored. This has food hygiene and food safety implications, not just for that child but for others in the same session. Possible sources of funding include: your local authority, sponsorship from a local supermarket or grocer and the Food Education Trust. There may also be some local charity bursaries available. See 'Food hygiene and risks' below for why this is important and explain to your SLT.

Local suppliers or supermarkets?

Introducing cooking into your school curriculum provides an opportunity to involve children in understanding where their food comes from. Many school meals services now use local suppliers for fresh groceries and meat which you might be able to use too. Some of the activities linked to the recipes encourage the children to investigate industrial food production to increase their awareness. You could use a world map and chart the provenance of all the ingredients used.

Some ingredients, such as fresh herbs, could be grown at school on a window ledge; others may take longer and need a bucket of earth on a patio, or you may even be able to use some of the school garden or playing field if you have one. An enthusiastic gardener is a great benefit. Perhaps one of the parents is itching to have an allotment and you could share a corner of the grounds of the school or put some tubs on a patio space in return for a growing teaching resource!

Storage containers for food. Use lidded plastic boxes for dry goods like flour and identify a clean, dry cupboard where they can be stored. Ideally store as little food as you can to be sure that it is free from any contamination or spoilage (and there is less chance of someone 'borrowing' your ingredients!). You will also need access to a fridge and occasionally may need some space in a freezer. Both should be regularly cleaned and have the temperatures checked by leaving a thermometer inside (available from supermarkets and hardware stores). Log the temperatures on a record sheet when you are using them. A fridge should be at around 4°C and a freezer at -18°C.

Storage containers for equipment. Look for lidded wipe clean storage boxes that you can stack. Lots of smaller boxes are more useful than one large one as you can just pick out the equipment you need for each recipe. For extra cleanliness, you can seal the boxes with food wrap film, especially over holiday periods, to stop dust getting in.

Somewhere to wash up. Even if you teach the children to wash up you will still want to go back through it and check. Children can use washing-up bowls set on tables, one with hot soapy water and one with rinsing water and then space to dry and stack, like a production line. Nominate a quality controller or two to make sure everything is washed properly. See if you can use the staffroom dishwasher, or the industrial dishwasher in the school kitchen. If access to both is difficult, you could consider reducing your washing up by using paper plates and bowls for setting out ingredients.

First aid kit. Check with the member of staff responsible for first aid for the location and inform them of the type of equipment you will be using.

Food hygiene and risks

Find out whether a member of staff has Food Hygiene training at Level 2. Or you can train on line (about £30) or contact your local Environmental Health Department, RSPH (Royal Society for Public Health) or The D&T Association. Training will help you identify where and when you or the children may be at risk during food activities and help you stay safe and healthy.

If you are sourcing the ingredients yourself you can guarantee the quality and safety. Get ingredients from a reputable supplier and then store correctly. There needs to be space in a clean fridge at the correct temperature and a regular check of dates on packaging. This fridge ideally needs to be identified as for the use of food activities only, not general staff use, to ensure that the cleanliness and hygiene is maintained and reduce risk of cross contamination while you are using it. Make a habit of writing on a packet the date it is opened and seal in a plastic bag or box.

Cooked meat, milk and eggs, shellfish, cooked rice, soft cheeses and prepared salads are classed as high risk food for food poisoning, so bear this in mind when shopping. Ideally buy fresh ingredients on the day you will use them rather than storing for a few days. Always take a cool bag and ice blocks with you if buying chilled or frozen food to keep it as cold as possible between the shop and the school fridge or freezer.

Getting Started (cont)

Best practice

Children will copy your good habits, and your bad habits too! So start showing the children the safest and healthiest way of handling food from the outset. Use the Bridge and Claw holds when cutting even if you are using a table knife on soft cooked apples. The children will learn to have their fingers in the right place ready for when you introduce sharp knives when they are older (Photo 1). See video guides to help you with these and many other skills on the Food A Fact Of Life website: www.foodafactoflife.org.uk, The D&T Association website: www.data.org.uk and Children's Food Trust website: www.childrensfoodtrust.org.uk.

The two spoon method is used to transfer mixtures from the mixing bowl to the cooking container. You would usually use two dessert or tablespoons, loading one up with mixture and holding the second in your other hand to push the mixture off the spoon. We try to use the tools you already have to hand on the table (and are already dirty) to do this rather than using more equipment (Photo 2).

Spoon measures are often used in recipes. All spoon measures will be level unless specifically stated. To get good spoon measures of dry ingredients we suggest deep bowls; you will need additional quantities so the children can load the spoon easily. If measuring liquid, the spoon needs to be filled properly for a full measure. Do this by tipping the jug at an angle, lift your elbow, then put the level spoon into the liquid and it will fill (see cover photo). All the recipes are robust enough to allow for variations and inaccuracy so every child succeeds.

Discard food that has been on the floor. If one of the children drops their recipe, you can swap yours and the child will still be able to complete the recipe. Wash all fruit and vegetables before using them and explain that this removes dust, dirt and surface chemicals.

If ingredients are shared and handled, such as black pepper, this should be thrown away after each session as multiple fingers will have potentially contaminated it.

Break eggs individually into a cup or mug. Show the children that they need both hands and that the egg will try to escape or jump out of the shell. Explain that the yolk should be plump and the white clear. Use a teaspoon or clean hands to remove any stray shell (Photo 3).

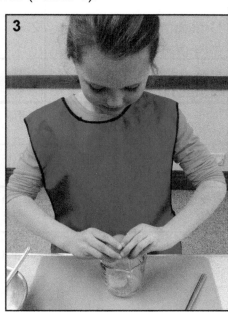

Index of frequently used ingredients

Baking powder	This raising agent starts to work as soon as it gets wet, so mixtures need to get into the oven fairly swiftly after putting together (if possible) to optimise the results.
Black pepper	We use fine ground black pepper.
Butter	All the recipes use salted butter unless otherwise stated. The small amount of salt in butter can help enhance the flavour. Additional salt is only used in bread. Various **non-dairy alternatives** are available, usually sold in 500g packs. Butter can be replaced by a **spreading margarine** but do not use light versions as the water content may impact on the result of your recipe. Check on labelling that it is suitable for baking/cooking.
Butter – melted	A number of recipes may call for melted butter. If you do not have access to a microwave or hob to prepare this then butter can be melted in a bowl partially immersed in boiling water, well away from the children. Use a good conductive material such as metal or glass to help the process. Once melted, butter will remain hot and liquid for some time. Non-dairy alternatives are suitable.
Cheese	Many of the recipes call for cheddar style hard cheese. If you buy mature or extra mature you get lots more flavour for the same fat content as mild cheese. If grated hard cheese is required, and the children are going to grate it, then it is easier if the cheese is at room temperature. This makes grating safer as the cheese is softer. However they will need a slightly larger piece so they have the correct amount and some additional cheese to hold onto. **Non-dairy hard cheese** alternatives are available. **Soft Cheese** is available as full fat or low fat versions. It contains **cow's milk**. A **lactose free** version is widely available, and a **non-dairy version** is available from some large supermarkets or specialist health food shops. It usually comes in 200g, 250g or 300g packs so can often be measured straight from the pack without weighing. This cheese handles best when slightly warm, so take out of the fridge about 15 minutes before you use it.
Eggs	All recipes are tested using medium eggs. Breaking eggs is a two handed job: one to firmly hold the egg and one to firmly hold the container, eg cup/mug. Use clean fingers or a teaspoon to remove stray egg shell.
Flour	All the recipes have been tested using wheat flour. Gluten free alternatives are available and produce good results unless otherwise stated, eg Quick Yeast Bread Rolls. We do not sieve the flour in any of the recipes as we have found no appreciable difference to the results. If flour looks lumpy then stir through with a fork to open up the grains. Self-raising flour has the raising agent, ie baking powder, already blended in. Standard flour comes in 1.5kg or 500g bags. Gluten free or specialist flour may be in 1kg bags.
Fresh fruit	Where a recipe calls for fresh fruit it is a good idea to buy ahead to get the fruit to soften and ripen ready. Putting a banana in with the fruit in a folded paper bag can help speed up the process. Always wash fruit. **Frozen fruit** can be very juicy but is a good source when not in season and may reduce your preparation time. It may need patting dry with kitchen paper once defrosted. **Tinned Fruit**: look for versions packed with natural juice, some are packed in syrup which contains additional sugar which is not needed. The tin will give a total weight and a drained weight, so use the drained weight to calculate how many tins to buy. Drain tinned fruit well then dry on kitchen paper to remove excess liquid, unless otherwise instructed. **Tinned apples** are generally tightly packed without juice. Tinned fruit is an ideal store cupboard ingredient to have to hand.

Know Your Equipment

We have devised these recipes to use as few pieces of equipment as possible. You may decide to invest in some 'nice to have' items such as spatulas to make it easier to transfer a mixture from the mixing bowl to the cooking container, but as it is not essential we may have not listed it as so. The key is to have as few barriers to undertaking a cooking activity as possible so that when the recipe goes home the parents and children will be able to repeat the recipe again and again.

The most used items for these recipes:

Aprons	One for every child in the group and all adults taking part; we have found tabards very useful. Keep them exclusively for food use. Alternatively use disposable.
Baking tray	Use it as a tray to load up with multiple cooking containers to transport safely to the oven. Also use in the oven and for removing from the oven for the same reason. Line with paper to save washing up!
Baking parchment/paper	We use parchment as it is non-stick, ideal for keeping baking trays clean and is easy to write on to name children's cooking with a permanent, non-toxic marker pen.
Cooking container	The recipes in this book call for 400ml foil containers with lids which can be purchased in bulk from the cash and carry or most supermarkets. You can score the bottom of the foil with the child's name, or write on the lid, to ensure that the child gets back their own cooking. They can be used in the freezer, fridge and oven but not the microwave. Some recipes refer to a clear plastic deli pot – the type that you would buy olives or ready made salad in at a salad bar. These are available from cash and carry shops.
Cutlery 	Look for handle comfort and grip. You will need table knives, forks and spoons. Spoons may be used to measure both liquids and solids. You don't need to buy specific measuring spoons; in fact these can be awkward for children to hold. Use conventional domestic cutlery for ease and economy. As a guide a **teaspoon** (tsp) will measure about 5ml, a **dessertspoon** (dsp) will measure about 10ml and a **tablespoon** (tbsp) will measure about 15ml. Tablespoons are often available in separate packs or individually in the cutlery section of stores and cash and carry shops. All our recipes use level or flat spoon measures unless otherwise stated. Cutlery may be available to borrow from your school dining room.
Cutters	If making a recipe such as Tomato and Cheese Scones, all the children need to use the same size cutter so that the scones cook in the same time. Tin ones tend to rust so plastic is recommended.
Grater 	This must be sharp to be safe as it will cut more easily. For younger children we like the safe grater with a suction pad underneath that sticks the grater to the work surface and a pushing block to guide the food. Provide a fork to help the children get the gratings out without the use of their fingers. For older children we use a pyramid grater with rubber non-slip feet. Pyramid graters can be carefully bashed on the work mat to release the gratings (or a fork used on the inside). When using a grater, place a piece of damp kitchen roll under the work mat to stop it from slipping.

Weighing scales 	For speedy pre-weighing and for use with older children (7 plus), use electronic scales. Keep a set exclusively for food use and have a spare set of batteries ready to hand. For younger children use balance scales with metric weights which the children can handle to feel the mass before the ingredient is weighed in the pan. Check the calibration as they should balance when empty. The pan can be lined with food film to save on washing up! There are also spring style scales where the pan is on top of the gauge. These often weigh up to large amounts such as 2–3kg. This means that the scale is not very sensitive to the smaller quantities of ingredients in this book so accuracy is compromised and they are unsuitable for the children to use.
Work mat	A dishwasher safe thin plastic mat used for light chopping and cutting, ideally between A4 and A3 in size. These are ideal to help define the working area for each cook and can be kept very clean. Wrap sets in film wrap when they come out of the dishwasher to keep them clean for next time. To stop the mat from slipping on the table top, use a damp piece of kitchen roll or thin unwoven dishcloth underneath which will act as a brake. Industry standard colour coded mats used to reduce the risk of cross contamination: • blue for raw fish • red for raw meat • white for dairy or bakery • green for vegetables • brown for salads and fruit • yellow for cooked meats Please note: a blue mat is used in the photographs in this book simply to enhance the clarity of the ingredients, equipment and layout. This does not reflect the cooking/food preparation standard.

Additional equipment:

Garlic press	Usually made in metal, it crushes garlic cloves efficiently by forcing them through a grid of small holes, usually with some type of piston. Alternatively you can place the garlic clove in to a food safe plastic bag and bash it with a rolling pin.
Hob 	Plug in 3-pin socket hobs are widely available; induction hobs are more costly. Gas hobs are not suitable for indoor use (check PAC testing of any new equipment you purchase).
Kettle	Make sure that, if you are not using one from school, it has been PAC tested.

Plastic lidded pots	Useful for setting out ingredients as the lid ensures reduction of contamination while waiting. Also useful for handing out numerous ingredients, as well as used in a couple of recipes.
Pastry brush	Available in silicone which last longer than wooden versions especially if you plan to put them in a dishwasher. They are used for preparing the cooking container. Alternatively use butter and paper or just fingers!
Small sharing bowls	For small quantities such as ground black pepper and baking powder. Providing sufficient but limited amounts avoids contamination of all the stock.
Spatula	Silicone spatulas are very useful for hot and cold mixtures. When sourcing spatulas consider the size and length of the handle so it is appropriate for the age range that will be using them.
Whisk	Plain metal versions are best, but a fork, or 2 forks held together, can be just as satisfactory.
Wooden spoon	Look for short handled spoons which are suitable for all the children to use. Wash in warm soapy water and rinse. Dry well, you can put them in a cooling oven to get fully dry.

Risk Assessment: session specific

Completed form needed for each recipe

Session:

Room:

Recipe Name: Carrot Cake

Dates:

	Name	Action
Allergies	Unity – dairy (egg is OK)	Dairy free recipe so suitable
Intolerances	Shelli – no citrus fruits	Omit orange extract and zest. Replace with vanilla extract
Religious Considerations	none	

Recipe/session	Hazard	Persons at risk	Risk Low/Medium/High	Control Measures
Carrot Cake	Grater – finger ends can be caught in grater	Children	Low	Always use sharp graters as less pressure is required. Place damp cloth under work mat to reduce chances of grater slipping. Clear demonstration of technique given – grater facing away.

Name: _____

Signed: _____

Date: _____ **Position in School:** _____

Additional Comments:

Pro-forma Allergy/Intolerance/Religious/ Lifestyle Consideration Form (adapt to your own needs)

Dear

You have said that your child (name)_____
has a food allergy, intolerance, religious or lifestyle consideration which may
have an effect on their practical food activities in school.

To help us make sure that cooking is an enjoyable and safe activity for your
child and help us to provide alternatives, please complete the following
form and return to school so that your child can take part in the activity on

_____.

(Please delete/fill in the information below, where appropriate, and sign.)
Intolerance / allergy to_____

This is results in (hives, vomiting, tummy ache....please give details)
_____

He / she last ate this food _____

He / she last saw a doctor about this when?_____

We have / have not had a specialist referral concerning this reaction.

We do the following (avoid / don't eat / have an epipen ....please give details)
_____
_____

If an Epipen is used, where is this stored?_____

Due to religious or lifestyle considerations we would like our child not to handle
or eat the following ingredients; _____
_____
_____

I, (name)_____
am aware that the school will do everything within their control to respond to
the information given and that this information will be used with discretion.

Signature: _____

Date: _____

Recipe type and cross-curricular links

	Dips	Wrap Sandwiches	Tomato & Cheese Scones	Highland Pudding	Ginger & Pineapple Cheesecake	Potato Omelette	Savoury Bread & Butter Pudding	Saucy Fish Pie	Fruit Crumble	Peach & Cherry Upside-Down Cake	Macaroni Cheese	Quick Yeast Bread Rolls	Couscous Salad	Pear Tear & Share	Carrot Cake
Computing				✓		✓		✓				✓		✓	
PSHE			✓					✓			✓		✓		
Art		✓								✓					
History															✓
Geography	✓			✓				✓							
Science			✓			✓	✓				✓	✓	✓		
Language & Literacy					✓			✓							✓
Maths	✓	✓				✓	✓							✓	
D & T	✓	✓	✓	✓	✓	✓	✓	✓	✓	✓	✓	✓	✓	✓	✓
Non cook	✓	✓		✓	✓							✓			
Hob						✓		✓			✓				
Oven			✓			optional	✓	✓	✓	✓		✓		✓	✓
Vegetarian option	✓	✓	✓	✓	✓	✓	✓		✓	✓	✓	✓	✓	✓	✓
Savoury	✓	✓	✓			✓	✓	✓			✓	✓	✓		
Sweet				✓	✓				✓	✓				✓	✓
Page	30	34	38	42	46	50	54	58	62	66	70	74	78	82	86
Key Stage	Key Stage 1	Key Stage 1	Key Stage 1	Key Stage 1	Key Stage 1	Lower Key Stage 2	Lower Key Stage 2	Lower Key Stage 2	Lower Key Stage 2	Lower Key Stage 2	Upper Key Stage 2	Upper Key Stage 2	Upper Key Stage 2	Upper Key Stage 2	Upper Key Stage 2

Dips

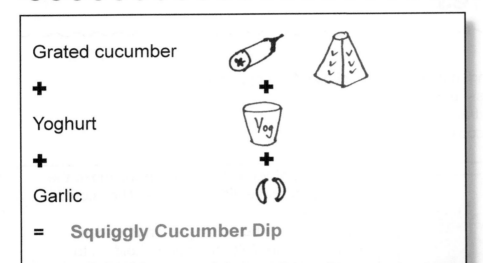

Grated cucumber

+

Yoghurt

+

Garlic

= **Squiggly Cucumber Dip**

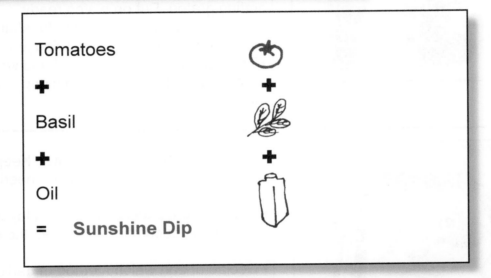

Tomatoes

+

Basil

+

Oil

= **Sunshine Dip**

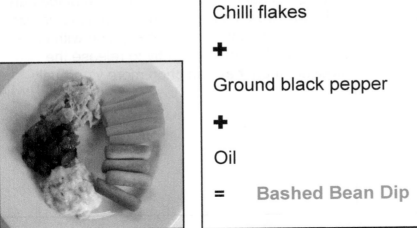

Cannellini beans

+

Chilli flakes

+

Ground black pepper

+

Oil

= **Bashed Bean Dip**

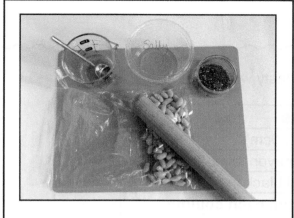

Bashed Bean Dip:
• Use freezer bags as they are a thicker gauge and more resilient for bashing than sandwich bags. Bashing can be noisy – make sure the tables are strong enough for enthusiastic bashing and keep equipment on the table to a minimum to avoid things falling off. The beans need to be well squashed for them to form a paste consistency.
• Adding all the ingredients to the bag saves on washing up!

Skill Up
Children prepare some carrot sticks by peeling and cutting into batons to serve with the dips (upper KS2).

Skill down
Use tinned tomatoes instead of fresh for the Sunshine Dip; omit the Squiggly Cucumber Dip recipe as an option.

Adapting the recipe for dietary/religious considerations

The following substitutions can be made (see also Know Your Ingredients, pages 16–18):

Reason	Substitute	With
dairy allergy	natural yoghurt	soya natural yoghurt

Safety advice

Cover and refrigerate the dips if they are not being eaten immediately. **Eat within 48 hours.**

If eating and sharing the dips, show children how to dip once and eat one bread stick/carrot stick at a time to reduce the risk of sharing their oral bacteria with others (double dipping is where you dip something that has already been in the mouth – such as a tasting spoon – allowing oral bacteria into the mixture).

Getting more out of your food practical session

D&T – What food groups are in the dip you made?

Geography – Where do the ingredients in the dips come from? Can you locate the countries on a map of the world?

Maths (measuring) – practice measuring by weight (g) and volume (ml) with activities.

Wrap Sandwiches

Mayonnaise

+

Ground black pepper

+

Chicken, cheese or tuna

+

Tomato, grated carrot or fresh pepper

+

Baby spinach or lettuce

+

Wrap

+

Fridge

=

Wrap Sandwich

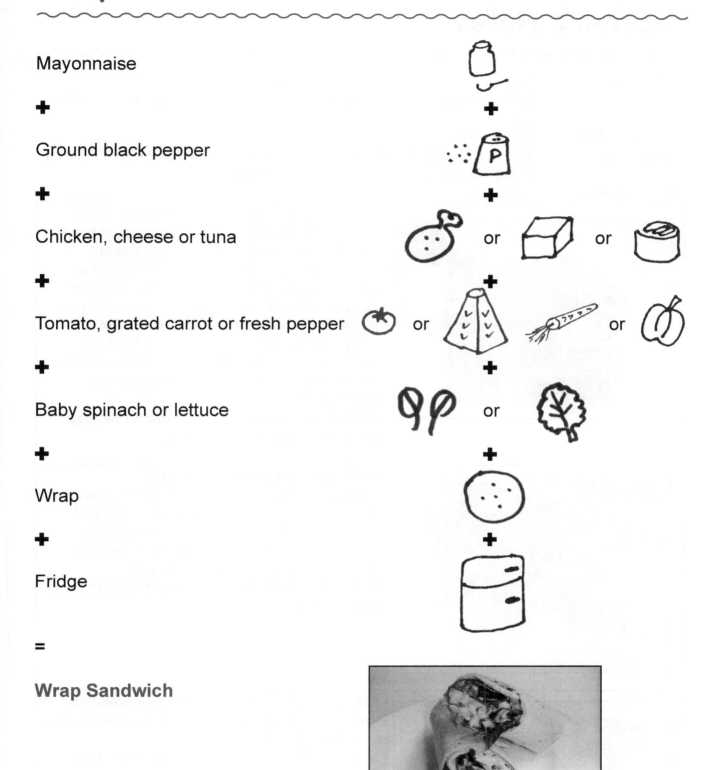

• Position ingredients as shown. Roll up tightly to enclose the filling and tuck the ends of the rolled wrap in to avoid any filling falling out.
• Cut in half. You will need to do this for KS1 as a sharp knife is needed to cut through the layers.
• A cocktail stick can be used to secure the wrap.

Skill up
Use a sharp knife with bridge hold (Upper KS2) to cut the tomatoes.

Skill down
Reduce ingredients to one combination and use pre-grated cheese.

Adapting the recipe for dietary/religious considerations

The following substitutions can be made (see also Know Your Ingredients, pages 16–18):

Reason	Substitute	With
wheat/gluten allergy	wraps	gluten free wraps (available from specialist food shops and some supermarkets)
dairy allergy	cheddar cheese	non-dairy hard cheese
egg allergy	mayonnaise	check for egg content or replace with natural yoghurt

Safety advice

Wrap in cling film/foil/food bag and refrigerate. **Eat on the day you make them.**
Take special care if handling cooked meat to wash hands and equipment thoroughly.

Getting more out of your food practical session

D&T – Design your own filling using the Eatwell plate (page 9) as a guide so that you include ingredients from a number of food groups (see choices in the recipe).

Maths – The wrap starts as a circle and becomes a cylinder. What shapes do other foods come in?

Art – Design a wrapper to tie around the wrap you have made.

Tomato and Cheese Scones

Flour

+

Butter

+

Basil

+

Tomato purée

+

Ground black pepper

+

Milk

+

Grated cheese

+

Oven

=

Tomato and Cheese Scones

10–12 mins

• Cheese can be provided ready grated. If you provide a block of cheese, weigh a little extra to allow for wastage as the children will need something to hold on to!

Skill up
Allow the children to carry out all the processes themselves (KS2) and cut herbs with a sharp knife.

Skill down
Provide ready grated cheese and pre-weighed flour and butter in individual bowls.

Adapting the recipe for dietary/religious considerations

The following substitutions can be made (see also Know Your Ingredients, pages 16–18):

Reason	Substitute	With
wheat/gluten allergy	self-raising flour	gluten free self-raising flour
dairy allergy	cheddar cheese	non-dairy hard cheese
	milk	dairy free milk
	butter	dairy free margarine

Safety advice

Allow scones to cool before splitting to reduce risk of scalding. These do not need chilling, store in a food bag/box. **Eat fresh on the day you make them.**

Getting more out of your food practical session

D&T – How should you cut out the dough so that you don't have to re-roll the mixture more than once?

Science – An investigation. What is in self raising flour? Why do the scones rise in the oven and get bigger?

PSHE – Write an invitation to a picnic where you could share your scones with friends.

Highland Pudding

Yoghurt

+

Honey

= Yoghurt mix

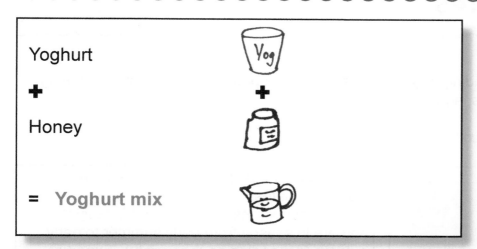

Layer 1

Raspberries

+

Yoghurt mix

+

Oats

Layer 2

Raspberries

+

Yoghurt mix

+

Oats

+

Fridge

=

Highland Pudding

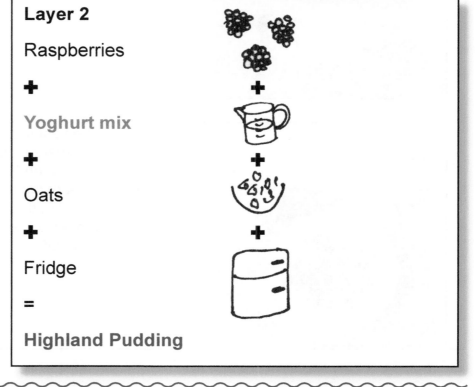

• You assemble the pudding by using half the fruit and half the yoghurt in two layers. This is a very practical, visual use of maths language.
• Ask what will happen to the oats, especially the ones in the middle of the pudding? (They go soft and chewy.)

Skill up
Toast some of the oats in the oven to add to the topping for a crunchy finish (KS2).

Skill down
Provide all the ingredients pre-measured so children concentrate on the measure or estimation of half.

Adapting the recipe for dietary/religious considerations

The following substitutions can be made (see also Know Your Ingredients, pages 16–18):

Reason	Substitute	With
wheat/gluten allergy	oats	gluten free oats
dairy allergy	natural yoghurt	soya natural yoghurt

Safety advice

Cover and keep refrigerated after making. **Eat within 48 hours.**

Getting more out of your food practical session

D&T – What sort of container is suitable for making your Highland Pudding in and why?

Computing – Rewrite the instructions for assembling the pudding in simple language to show how the two layers are identical and could be carried out by a robot.

Geography – This recipe is based on a traditional Scottish one called Cranachan. On a map of the UK, name and mark where the four countries that make up the United Kingdom are. Where do you live? Mark this on the map too. Where might the ingredients have grown/ been made?

Ginger and Pineapple Cheesecake

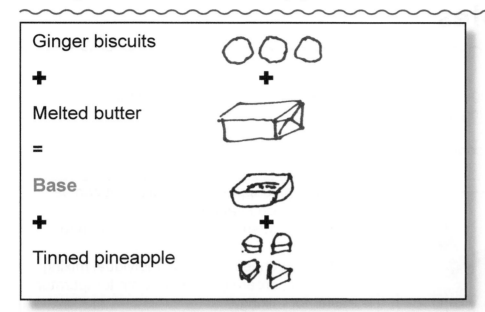

Ginger biscuits

+

Melted butter

=

Base

+

Tinned pineapple

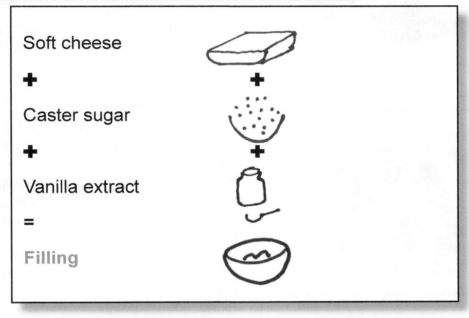

Soft cheese

+

Caster sugar

+

Vanilla extract

=

Filling

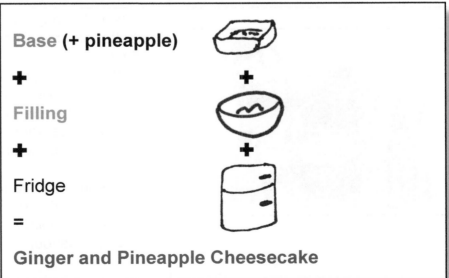

Base (+ pineapple)

+

Filling

+

Fridge

=

Ginger and Pineapple Cheesecake

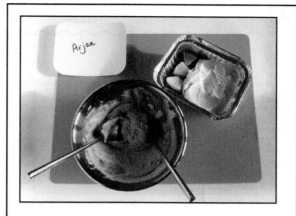

• Tip: Take care when putting the cheese mix over the fruit layer as you don't want to disturb the fruit so the two spoon method is vital. Instruct children not to stir otherwise the fruit pattern will be disturbed.

Skill up
Use fresh fruit such as a ripe nectarine and prepare with a sharp knife (KS2).

Skill down
Pre-set the biscuits in the bags ready for bashing and hand out the measured amount of butter.

Adapting the recipe for dietary/religious considerations

The following substitutions can be made (see also Know Your Ingredients, pages 16–18):

Reason	Substitute	With
wheat/gluten/dairy allergy	ginger biscuits	gluten free and dairy free alternative biscuits
dairy allergy	soft cheese	dairy free soft cheese (available from specialist shops and larger supermarkets)

Safety advice

Cover and keep refrigerated after making. **Eat within 48 hours.**

Getting more out of your food practical session

D&T - Design and make a box out of card that you could take your cheesecake home in or you could test different materials to see which are suitable for cake boxes

Science – Reversible and irreversible changes - put butter and chocolate for example on the radiator. What happens when they are heated?

Literacy – Describe the sequence of how you made the cheesecake to someone, you could record this and listen back to see how clear you were.

Potato Omelette (Frittata)

Spring onion

+

Cooked potato

+

Mushrooms

+

Grated cheese

+

Herbs

+

Eggs

+

Ground black pepper

+

Hob

= **Potato Omelette**

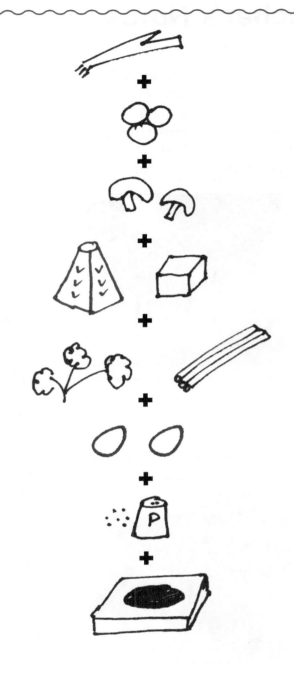

• Show breaking the egg individually into a separate container, eg a cup, before you add it, so that it can be checked for freshness and any pieces of shell. Use a teaspoon or a clean finger to remove any shell.

Skill up
Use raw potatoes (waxy variety). Peel and cook them in a separate saucepan. Use a white onion and soften in the pan with the mushrooms then add the egg, potato and herbs (Upper KS2).

Skill down
Tear the mushrooms. Oven bake instead of using the hob. Combine all the ingredients, add to a lightly oiled foil container and bake in the oven (180°C fan/200°C/Gas 6) for about 15–20 minutes.

Adapting the recipe for dietary/religious considerations

The following substitutions can be made (see also Know Your Ingredients, pages 16–18):

Reason	Substitute	With
egg allergy	This recipe is not suitable for children with egg allergies.	
dairy allergy	cheddar cheese	non-dairy hard cheese

Safety advice

Cover and keep refrigerated after making. **Eat within 48 hours.**

Getting more out of your food practical session

D&T – Where do eggs come from? How do they get from the farm to the shop?

Science – How does canning preserve food? (tinned potatoes) What other ways are foods preserved?

Computing – Where does the dish Frittata originate? Research dishes served at school and find out where they originate from, eg lasagne, cheesecake.

Savoury Bread and Butter Pudding

Bread

+

Butter

+

Sausages

+

Bacon

+

Tomato

+

Egg

+

Milk

+

Ground black pepper

+

Grated cheese

+

Oven

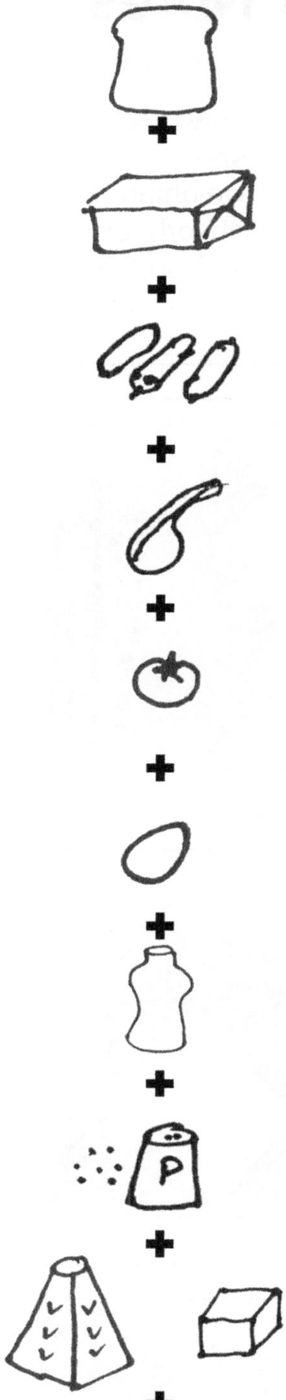

20–25 mins

= Savoury Bread and Butter Pudding

- The milk and egg mixture is an egg custard.
- When tipping the liquid onto the bread layers take care as it may splash back.
- Once all the liquid is added, gently press the bread down with the fork to help the top layer absorb it.

Skill up
Children do all processes and grate the cheese. Children have supervised use of the oven.

Skill down
Use baby tomatoes that can be chopped in the jug with scissors.

Adapting the recipe for dietary/religious considerations

The following substitutions can be made (see also Know Your Ingredients, pages 16–18):

Reason	Substitute	With
egg allergy	This recipe is not suitable for children with egg allergies.	
dairy allergy	milk and butter	non-dairy versions work well
	cheddar cheese	non-dairy hard cheese
gluten allergy	bread	gluten free bread
vegetarian	bacon, cocktail sausages	vegetarian meat replacements, mushrooms or sweetcorn
no pork products due to religious considerations	bacon, cocktail sausages	other cooked meat such as chicken or vegetarian meat replacements

Safety advice

If you are using cooked meats then ensure that it is kept cool before use and take special care to wash hands and equipment thoroughly. Once made, allow the pudding to cool then cover and keep refrigerated. **Eat within 48 hours.**

Getting more out of your food practical session

D&T – How is bread manufactured – from the field to the shop?

Maths – Triangles and angles

Science – What conditions do you need to grow tomatoes? Try to grow your own.

Saucy Fish Pie

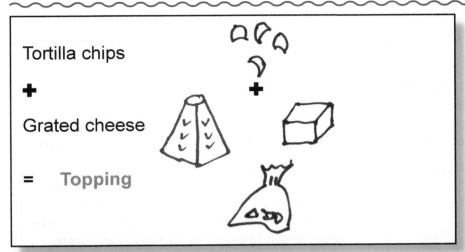

Tortilla chips

+

Grated cheese

= Topping

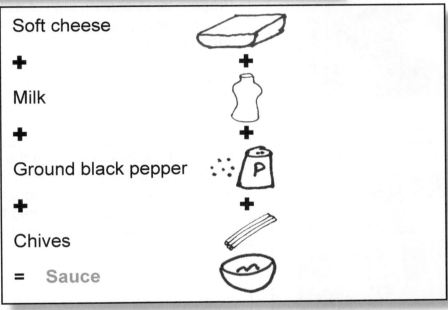

Soft cheese

+

Milk

+

Ground black pepper

+

Chives

= Sauce

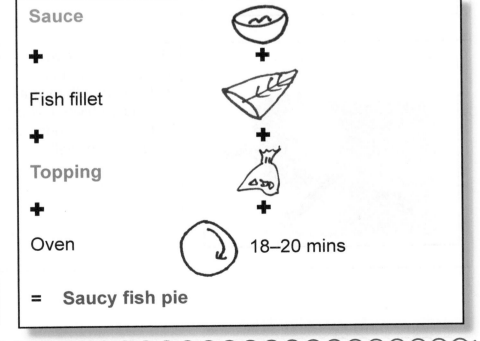

Sauce

+

Fish fillet

+

Topping

+

Oven   18–20 mins

= Saucy fish pie

- Prepare the fish using the claw hold with the fingers tucked under the knuckles. Add to the sauce and stir gently until all the fish is covered.
- Assemble the dish whilst your hands are still sticky. Then instruct the children to wash their hands thoroughly (raw fish).
- Once cooked, use a temperature probe to check that the reading is a minimum of 63°C, or cut into the centre of your demonstration version to check the fish is cooked.

Skill up
Get the children to measure all the ingredients and grate the cheese themselves (Upper KS2).

Skill down
Have milk ready measured in jugs and use scissors for herbs and fish.

Adapting the recipe for dietary/religious considerations

The following substitutions can be made (see also Know Your Ingredients, pages 16–18):

Reason	Substitute	With
dairy allergy	milk and soft cheese	non-dairy versions available
	cheddar cheese	non-dairy hard cheese
gluten/wheat allergy	tortilla chips	wheat free tortilla chips (available from specialist shops and larger supermarkets)

Safety advice

As you are using raw fish, ensure that it is kept cool before use and take special care to wash hands and equipment thoroughly. If you are sending this dish home for cooking, prepare the topping and leave in the named bag. Refrigerate the uncooked pie. The cooked pie should also be refrigerated. **Eat on the day you make it.**

Getting more out of your food practical session

D&T – Identify ingredients in the Saucy Fish Pie that contain fat and offer suggestions as alternatives to reduce fat content of the recipe.

Geography – Fish in the oceans of the world. Name and locate the areas of ocean on the earth on a world map and find out about the types of fish that are caught there.

Computing – Create a web page/blog for the school website about why we should eat fish in a balanced diet.

Fruit Crumble

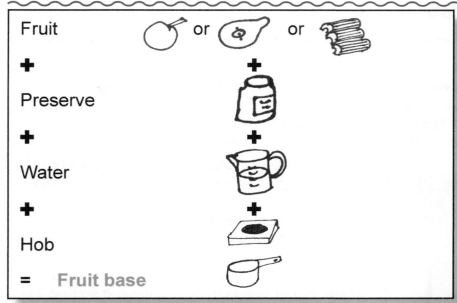

Fruit   or   or

+

Preserve

+

Water

+

Hob

=   Fruit base

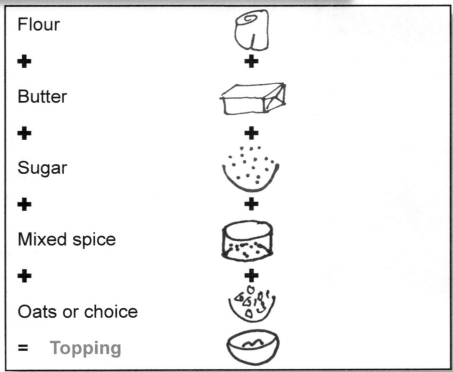

Flour

+

Butter

+

Sugar

+

Mixed spice

+

Oats or choice

=   Topping

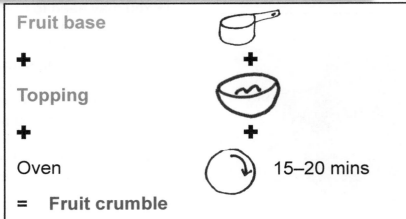

Fruit base

+

Topping

+

Oven   15–20 mins

=   **Fruit crumble**

- You could taste test the mixture for sweetness using a **clean** sppon.
- Tip the crumble topping onto the fruit – no stirring or patting down is needed.

Skill up

Ask the children to weigh the crumble topping. You could also introduce using the 'add and weigh' facility on digital scales.

Skill down

Use tinned fruit and cut with a table knife, then put straight into the cooking container and omit the hob skill. Teach bridge and claw hold, even if using a table knife.

Adapting the recipe for dietary/religious considerations

The following substitutions can be made (see also Know Your Ingredients, pages 16–18):

Reason	Substitute	With
dairy allergy	butter	non-dairy version available
gluten/wheat allergy	flour, oats, muesli and oaty biscuits	gluten free versions are available

Safety advice

Allow to cool thoroughly then chill. **Eat within 48 hours.** If you are sending this dish home for cooking, refrigerate the uncooked crumble.

Getting more out of your food practical session

D&T – Evaluate the different crumble combinations used in the class. Look at texture, colours and nutrition.

Language and Literacy – Create a language board with words you can use to describe the texture and flavour of different fruits .

PSHE – Organise a fruit tasting session for a group of people to encourage them to eat more fresh fruit and try new ones.

Peach and Cherry Upside-Down Cake

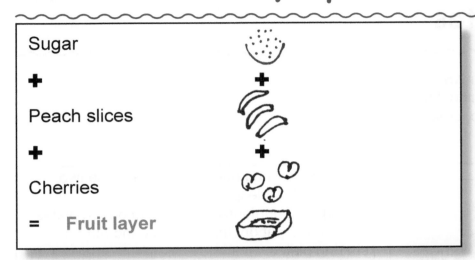

Sugar

+

Peach slices

+

Cherries

=   **Fruit layer**

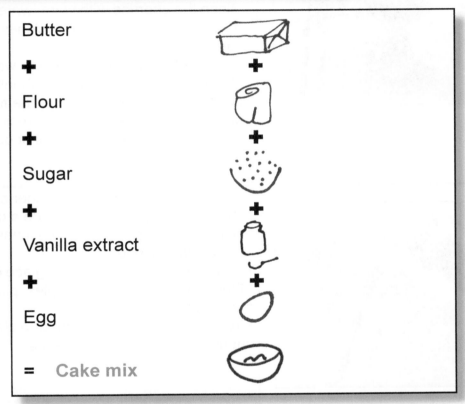

Butter

+

Flour

+

Sugar

+

Vanilla extract

+

Egg

=   **Cake mix**

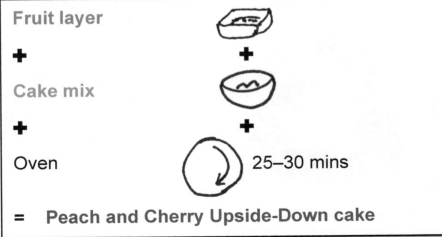

Fruit layer

+

Cake mix

+

Oven   25–30 mins

=   **Peach and Cherry Upside-Down cake**

• Use the 2 spoon method to scoop the mixture up then push off to place on top of the fruit layer.
• When the mixture is added on top of the fruit be careful not to disturb the pattern and don't stir!

Skill up
Children can prepare all the ingredients. Prepare fruit with a sharp knife and use bridge and claw holds (see Best Practice, page 15). Use an electric hand beater.

Skill down
Pre-weigh the dry ingredients for the children so they can concentrate on breaking the egg and making the fruit pattern.

Adapting the recipe for dietary/religious considerations

The following substitutions can be made (see also Know Your Ingredients, pages 16–18):

Reason	Substitute	With
egg allergy	Is this raw or cooked egg? Check with parent/carer. Investigate egg replacer.	
dairy allergy	butter	non-dairy version works well
gluten/wheat allergy	self-raising flour	gluten free self-raising flour

Safety advice

Leave to cool completely then seal in an air tight bag for going home. Do not store unused tinned fruit in the tins, decant into a labelled plastic bag or box and refrigerate or freeze to use another time. **Eat within 48 hours.**

Getting more out of your food practical session

D&T – What materials are cooking containers made from? Why do you think these are used?

Maths – Write a shopping list of the ingredients you would need to buy to make 3 cakes. (3 x each ingredient). Can you calculate how much it would cost? Give sample prices that suit the ability of your class.

Art – Design some patterns for the top of the cake using the shapes of different fruit.

Macaroni Cheese

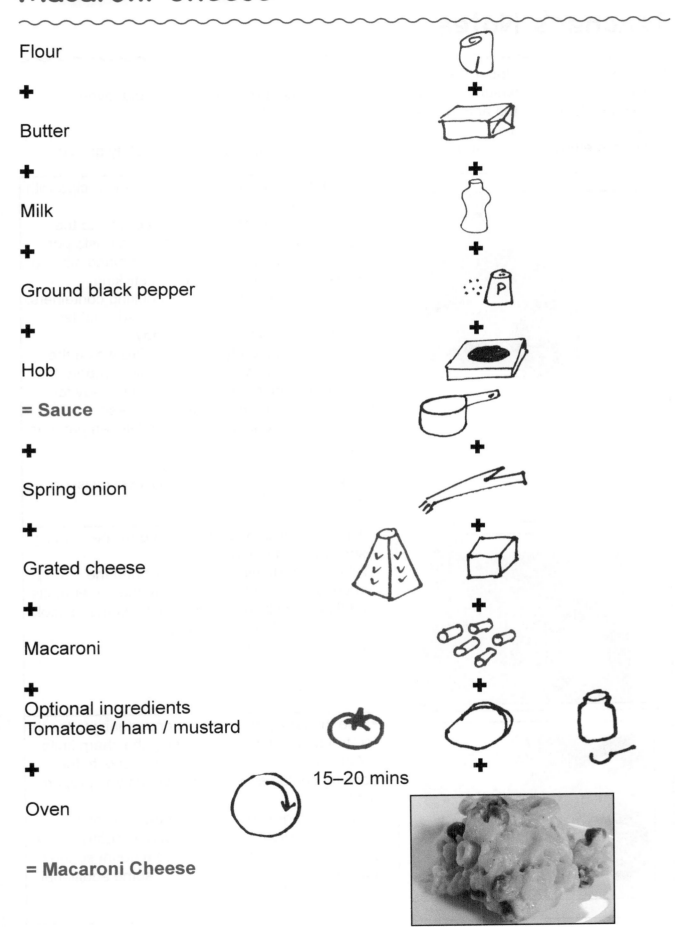

Flour

+

Butter

+

Milk

+

Ground black pepper

+

Hob

= Sauce

+

Spring onion

+

Grated cheese

+

Macaroni

+

Optional ingredients
Tomatoes / ham / mustard

+

Oven

15–20 mins

= Macaroni Cheese

- Tip the macaroni and other prepared ingredients from the cooking container into the saucepan of sauce, mix well, then return to the cooking container.
- Keep some of the cheese on one side to sprinkle on the top.
- You can use alternative shapes to macaroni such as penne and fusilli.

Skill up
Ask the children to cook the pasta in groups following the instructions (this will extend the preparation time and use more saucepans/hobs).

Skill down
Use scissors for onion preparation; use ready grated cheese.

Adapting the recipe for dietary/religious considerations

The following substitutions can be made (see also Know Your Ingredients, pages 16–18):

Reason	Substitute	With
dairy allergy	milk and butter	non-dairy versions
	cheddar cheese	non-dairy hard cheese
gluten/wheat allergy	flour and pasta	gluten free flour and pasta

Safety advice

If you are using meat, ensure that it is kept cool before use and take special care to wash hands and equipment thoroughly. Put the lid on the container, name and date then refrigerate. If cooking at school, allow to cool thoroughly then chill. This can go home uncooked if it is a meat free version. **Eat within 48 hours.**

Getting more out of your food practical session

D&T – What other pasta shapes could you use? Can you make pasta yourself?

Science – Explore the smell, taste and texture of your macaroni cheese using all your senses.

PSHE – Design a poster about how to use a hob or oven safely.

Quick Yeast Bread Rolls

Flour

+

Salt

+

Sugar

+

Dried yeast

+

Warm water

= **Dough**

+

Rosemary leaves

+

Sultanas

+

Oven

15–20 mins

= **Quick Yeast Bread Rolls**

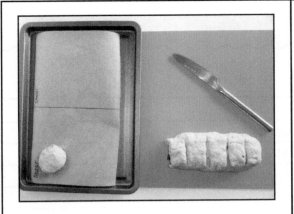

- Use the knife to mark up the 6 even sections before cutting – they need to be the same to cook in the same time.
- When positioning the dough balls on the tray allow for expansion in the oven!

Skill up
Use fresh yeast dissolved in water and watch the foam develop before using.

Skill down
Omit the flavour and make plain bread rolls.

Adapting the recipe for dietary/religious considerations

The following substitutions can be made (see also Know Your Ingredients, pages 16–18):

Reason	Substitute	With
gluten/wheat allergy	Not suitable for gluten free diet. Gluten free bread blend flour cannot be swapped into this recipe. However there are gluten free bread kits available.	

Safety advice

Be careful if boiling the water in the classroom/walking with hot water. **Eat fresh on the day you make them.**

Getting more out of your food practical session

D&T – Compare the ingredients on a packet of bought bread rolls with the ingredients you used for the recipe. What do the extra ingredients do?

Science – What conditions are needed for yeast to work? Carry out an experiment to demonstrate.

Computing – Create a cookery video to demonstrate the algorithm of the recipe.

Couscous Salad

Couscous

+

Boiling water (!)

+

Olive oil

+

Ground black pepper

+

Stock powder

+

Spice

+

Fresh pepper

+

Spring onion

+

Fresh coriander

+

any extra choices

+

Fridge

= **Couscous Salad**

- If you are designing your own couscous salad there are four groups to choose from:
  - A. Additional spices
  - B. Additional herbs
  - C. Cooked meat or dairy protein
  - D. Pulses for non-meat protein
- The last 2 groups turn the salad from a side dish into a main dish as it will contain a wider range of food groups, including protein. All are optional.
- Discuss how this recipe can use up lots of leftover cooked vegetables and meats to make another meal.

Skill up
Supervised but unaided use of the kettle.

Skill down
Have couscous ready, pre-weighed and cooled per child then demonstrate the preparation so they can see how it changes.

Adapting the recipe for dietary/religious considerations

The following substitutions can be made (see also Know Your Ingredients, pages 16–18):

Reason	Substitute	With
vegetarian	ham	non-meat alternative or omit
gluten/wheat allergy	couscous	rice noodles (crushed)
dairy allergy	feta cheese	non-dairy hard cheese

Safety advice

Be careful if boiling the water in the classroom/walking with hot water. If you are using cooked meat or tinned fish, fluff couscous up well to reduce the temperature then chill. Take special care to wash hands and equipment thoroughly afterwards. **Eat on the day you make it.**

Getting more out of your food practical session

D&T – Kettle design. Evaluate the different designs and materials used to make electric kettles and suggest the best and why. If you can, you could also compare the boiling times of different models.

Science – Couscous is a dehydrated food that absorbs water to become edible. Look at other foods that rely on evaporation and absorption.

PSHE – Investigate food wastage in the school canteen. Discuss with your class how they think this could be reduced and put the proposals to your teacher or the Head and the Head Chef.

Pear Tear and Share

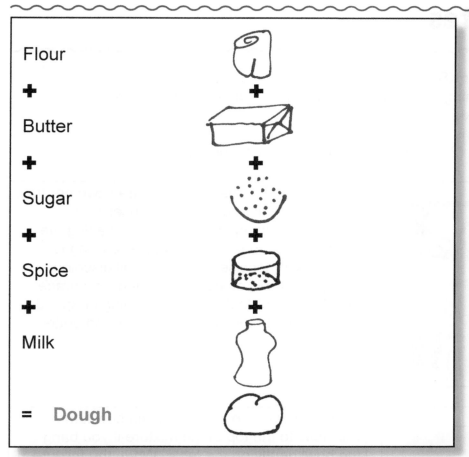

Flour

+

Butter

+

Sugar

+

Spice

+

Milk

= **Dough**

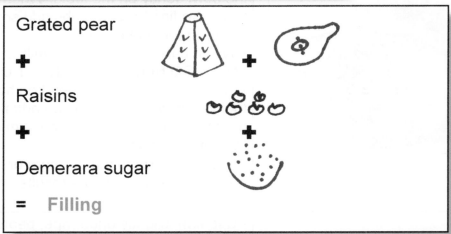

Grated pear

+

Raisins

+

Demerara sugar

= **Filling**

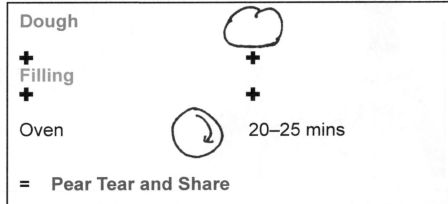

Dough

+

Filling

+

Oven   20–25 mins

= **Pear Tear and Share**

- Once the dough has been rolled out, ensure the filling is equally spread. Take care not to overfill.
- **Tip:** when cutting the spirals remember they need to all be the same size so they cook evenly.
- Then place all the spirals on the baking tray, cut side facing up. Ensure the raisins are hidden in the dough where possible otherwise they become overcooked and spoil.

Skill up
Ask the children to carry out the full recipe from scratch to see how much they can do on their own.

Skill down
Use tinned pear instead of fresh to remove the peeling process.

Adapting the recipe for dietary/religious considerations

The following substitutions can be made (see also Know Your Ingredients, pages 16–18):

Reason	Substitute	With
gluten/wheat allergy	self-raising flour	gluten free self-raising flour
dairy allergy	milk and butter	non-dairy versions

Safety advice

Wash sharp graters with care, use a fork to clean the fruit off the front. These do not need chilling, store in a food bag/box. **Eat fresh on the day you make them.**

Getting more out of your food practical session

D&T – Experiment with the shapes you can make your Pear Tear and Share in.

Maths – How much of the fruit do you use and how much is wasted? Calculate the wastage.

Computing – Find out the stages of creating an online grocery order from finding the web page to the payment page.

Carrot Cake

Flour

+

Baking powder

+

Sugar

+

Cranberries

+

Grated carrot

+

Egg

+

Vegetable oil

+

Orange zest/extract

+

Oven

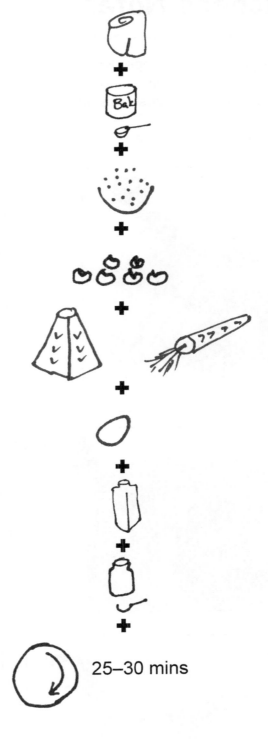

25–30 mins

= Carrot Cake

- Make sure the mixture is thoroughly mixed – pockets of flour sometimes collect in the dried fruit.
- Use the spoon to scoop and the fork to push the mixture into the container – 2 spoon method. As this mixture contains baking powder, once wet it will start reacting; cook as soon as you can, otherwise you can end up with a dense, rather than light cake

Skill up
Children use the add and weigh facility on digital scales to weigh the flour then add sugar into the same bowl. Use a hand mixer to mix together.

Skill down
Provide pre-grated carrot and offer only extract not zest.

Adapting the recipe for dietary/religious considerations

The following substitutions can be made (see also Know Your Ingredients, pages 16–18):

Reason	Substitute	With
gluten/wheat allergy	plain flour and baking powder	gluten free flour and baking powder
egg allergy	Is this raw or cooked egg? Check with parent/carer. Investigate egg replacer.	

Safety advice

Wash sharp graters with care, use a fork to clean the fruit off the front. These do not need chilling, store in a food bag/box. **Eat within 48 hours.**

Getting more out of your food practical session

D&T – Find other cake recipes that use vegetables in them.

Literacy – Write a poem about your favourite food.

History – Food was rationed during and after World War 2. Sugar was in short supply and carrots often replaced it in sweet recipes. Why was sugar difficult to get? Look at what a week's ration for a child your age would have been.